21st Century Leadership Guides

I0176575

May Your No Be a Yes

A Guide To Making Better Decisions

Dr. Ed Brenegar

An Imprint of Circle of Impact Press

21st Century Leadership Guides

An Imprint of Circle of Impact Press

May Your No Be A Yes:

A Guide To Making Better Decisions

ISBN (ebook): 978-1-7373097-0-3

ISBN (print): 978-1-7373097-1-0

Circle of Impact Press

North Wilkesboro, North Carolina

Published in the United States

Dedication

For Grandmere,

with honor and gratitude

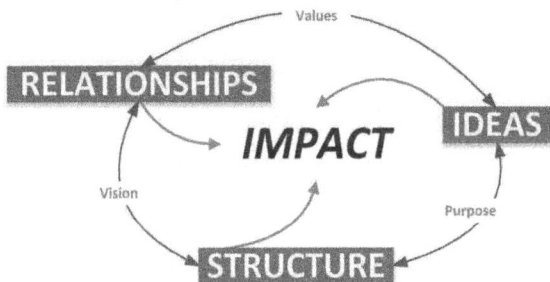

CIRCLE OF IMPACT
Taking Personal Initiative To Ignite Change

Values

RELATIONSHIPS

IDEAS

IMPACT

Vision

Purpose

STRUCTURE

Contents

Chapter One:
Saying No or Saying Yes

When a No is a No

Many years ago, I witnessed the end of a friend's marriage. Let's call him Jack, though that isn't his name. Jack wasn't sure what triggered the change in his wife's treatment of him. He was certain about when it began. There were accusations by his wife that he had lied to her about a purchase that she saw on a credit card statement. Then, there were accusations of failing to do things or be at a specific place as agreed. She accused him of saying things that he had no remembrance of saying. She finally accused him of failing to be a good husband and father.

Jack listened and tried to sort out where he had been wrong. He tried to accommodate. He tried to be better as a father and husband. During the middle of one of these tense moments of conflict, he realized that she was making it all up. That none of the situations that she described had happened. To her they were true. True as representative of the man she saw him to be.

Jack talked with me about the growing inability of he and his wife to communicate, to be intimate, and to manage their home. At that point, he began to say no. He challenged her accusations. He stood his ground. He didn't accuse in return. He just said, "No, it isn't true." As could be expected, the conflict between Jack and his wife increased. Within a short time, he moved out knowing that she was totally convinced in her own mind that she was right, the events she portrayed were true, and that she could never love such a man.

I have seen enough of these tragic situations to understand how they happen. I see in Jack's story the importance of knowing one's mind, of knowing what we believe and value. Before the conflict began, he was an easy-going, go-along-to-get-along kind of guy. This had always served him well socially and occupationally. Yet, the conflict with his wife changed Jack. He had to learn to stand up for himself. He had to learn to say No.

It was not easy for Jack because, like many people, he absorbed the expectations of the people around him. He conformed to them effortlessly. Everyone liked Jack, but no one really knew him. Jack was one of those nice guys who hang around the periphery of every group. Some people would call him a "Yes-man." It was only the growing intensity of emotional abuse by his wife that finally pushed him to change. He had to change or lose whatever sense of self-worth he had remaining.

I was acquainted with Jack's wife through various social encounters. Let's assume that Jack's perception of her treatment of him is an accurate description of his experience. I'm not interested in taking sides, of who is to blame for the demise of this marriage. They both are contributors. It is important to try and understand her perspective to fully appreciate how this marriage disintegrated in a matter of months. Let's look into her actions to understand why she changed in her behavior towards her husband. I will treat here as fairly and non-judgmentally as I will Jack. For many people, this is precisely the challenge that they have in relationships where there is a core conflict involved. People take one side or the other never understanding what happened to bring an end to a relationship that people once thought was ideal.

Jack's wife is Mary. When she met Jack, she thought him a perfect match. A good provider, attentive, and easy-going. As the family grew with two children within four years, Mary's attention to the family's needs grew. She found that she could not always depend on Jack to be available to take care of things. His work got in the way of his responsibilities to the family. One evening when Jack was out at a client dinner, she crossed a threshold of perception about him. He was no longer a fit match for her. He wasn't as attentive or dependable as he once was. She resolved in her mind to change him. In her mind, Mary had begun to say No to how her family was operating. She wanted more from her husband. She wanted him to be a better father to their children. Out of this shift in perception came the accusations that ultimately led to Jack moving out and a divorce settlement signed.

There is a two-sided problem that we can see in this story of Jack and Mary. We have a man who decides that he must begin to say No to emotionally survive a crumbling marriage. We have a woman who decides that she must say No in order for her family to survive what she perceives is a deteriorating situation.

What is missing from this relationship? It is easy to see that communication was missing. Jack and Mary lived together not so much as husband and wife, and father and mother, but as roommates sharing domestic responsibilities of a home and the raising of two children. This is not unlike a person finding the ideal place of employment, and then watching as the social environment of work changes. The responsibilities remain the same or increase, but the enjoyment of working for this company is gone. The same is true for Jack and Mary. Both learned to say No, but their No's were a response to something that they perceived as negative. Their No's were never about a specific Yes. Their No's were about survival in a situation that they each saw as unacceptable.

Communication in a marriage is dependent upon the couple nurturing intimacy in their relationship. This is especially true as the demands of family, children, and work grow. The natural intimacy that Jack and Mary knew as a young married couple could not be sustained except through attention given to their relationship as being as important as their individual desires as husband and wife, and parents of their two children.

"The days are long, the years are short."

Recently, Jean and I spent a day in an *Impact Day* planning session. The conversation that follows occurred a couple of hours into our session and represents the transition point in our day.

> Me: The idea ... is that you want every
> no that you make to be a yes towards

something that is important or valuable to you. … *you're saying no to affirm a yes.* … Does that make sense?

Jean: Yes.

Me: Why is that important to you?

Jean: Women are yes people, and we say yes to everything, and so we lose our purpose. Me: Do you lose your identity too?

Jean: Yeah.

This is the story I hear frequently. It is the floor of the house of personal stories. It is especially true for many women with whom I've talked and worked.

There is a difference between men and women here. I am open to being corrected. It isn't a difference in value. It's really a difference in experience and perception. It seems to me that men's purpose is driven much more towards task accomplishment. Women, like Jean and Mary, on the other hand, their purpose is much broader, encompassing the whole of their lives. It is much more relational.

It is an over-generalization, but it seems that men focus on the one thing that they need to do at that moment in time. It is hard to distract us when we are so focused. Is this the source of the complaint from women that we are not listening to them? Probably so, because in that moment, we aren't listening. We are focused on that one thing. Everything else is peripheral.

Women, however, see all the demands, all the responsibilities, all the priorities at the same time. For you, everything is a priority. You are experts at multi-tasking. It is a source of constant wonder for me. Yet, the problem that Jean is pointing towards is that if everything is a priority, then you live with a kind of tyranny of never feeling complete and finished.

My own experience and what I see in other men is that we can segment our attention, which gets translated into behaviors where we are intentionally ignoring people because they are not a priority at that moment. There is an inherent conflict here that requires a married couple establish intimacy and communication as a higher priority in order to meet the other obligations that they have.

Is it any wonder that Jack and Mary's relationship had such problems? Jack was making decisions that placed him in conflict with his family. His choice of a business meeting instead of some event with his kids was to Mary an intentional decision of choosing work over family. She triangulated the relationship that Jack had with her, to the family, and to his work. All three were priorities for him. Yet, she placed the family as the highest priority. A priority that Jack could never fulfill. The result is that conflict grew as the demands of family and work grew. Even learning to find a better balance between his work and family responsibilities, Jack could never fulfill the expectations that Mary had for him. Her expectations were born in an unfulfilled idealism that the reality of life did not diminish, but only made more urgent.

During the promotion tour for my book, Circle of Impact: Taking Personal Initiative To Ignite Change, people would come up to me and ask about the book. I would say, "… the book is for people in transition." I frequently heard stories like Jack and Mary's. Stories about how things were changing in that person's life. For them the transition was real, yet not at all clear.

To business people, I would say that "The Circle of Impact is a book for businesses in transition who want to elevate the leadership capacities of their people." In one of those instances, this is the conversation that transpired.

Me: What do you do?

Man: I head a support team for a group of software engineers.

Me: Does your team know WHY they are doing the work that they do? Man: Yeah, I think so.

Me: Do the software engineers respect the work that your team does for them?

*The guy turns towards me with a shocked look. Man: NO! They don't.

Me: Is your company clear about the impact that they are seeking to create? Man: I'm not sure of that.

In the amount of time it took to read that exchange, this guy's perception changed. His awareness shifted from a focus on his own role in the company to seeing a larger picture. His lack of awareness is a product of his focus.

If I could spend an Impact Day with him, we would expand his perception of what is happening with him, his work, and his family.

When I tell people that the Circle of Impact "is for people in transition." There is an immediate recognition. All I have to say is "Tell me about the transition that you are in." They describe a situation that they are in that "feels" like a transition. For those few minutes we have together, I show them how the Circle of Impact model can help them find clarity of understanding about their situation. That clarity leads to being able to say No which is a Yes.

In this sense, women are more self-aware than men. They are emotionally connected to a broad range of responsibilities that encompass their lives. Their challenge is discerning what priorities take precedent in the moment of awareness. Men are less self-aware because they focus on the essential task that fulfills the specific purpose of the moment. They too need discernment about what priority takes precedence at that moment. In this way, we are all alike.

As I listen to the women that I meet, I hear them talking about the full range of responsibilities that hold their attention. Many of them feel overwhelmed by the demands placed upon them. With men, it is very different. You have to catch them at the right moment for many to really hear you. We generally focus on a single thing at a time. It explains the popularity of books like Gary Keller's The One Thing and Greg McKeown's Essentialism. They help us to focus because most of us men are not multi-taskers. Yet, the complexity of life and work force it upon us. So, we too, like Jean are caught in circumstances where we need to say No to affirm a Yes.

Saying No to Say Yes

We each need to see how we can say No to affirm things of value that matter to us. The things that matter are things that we value. We value them because they connect us to values that define what matters to us. Our values are the ground on which we build our lives. Without clarity about our values, how can we say No that is a Yes. We don't really have Yes's.

In setting priorities, we need to have a clear under standing of our values and our sense of purpose. From this perspective, there is no distinction between people. We all need to learn to say No in order to affirm a Yes in our life.

Many of us grew up being people pleasers. It is a rather benign attitude where we want people to be happy. However, there is a deeper motivation to avoid conflict. This was Jack's dilemma as a go-along-to-get-along guy. Increasingly, there was nothing he could do to please Mary.

Was Jack responsible for her unhappiness? Or was it because she faced a severe conflict within herself. Her idealism acted as a guard against having to be vulnerable with people, including Jack. She could sit in judgment of people not meeting her standards, labeling them failures.

From this perspective, Jack could never be all that she wanted him to be. Her options were limited. Stay true to her impossible expectations for Jack and never find true happiness in marriage. Or admit that she is responsible for her own happiness and must accept this reality as the only alternative to the lonely life of an idealist.

This choice is not as clear as described. There is no simple right or wrong in this relationship. Both Jack and Mary carry the burden of the failure of their marriage. For Mary, her course of action, rightly or wrongly, was never going to change Jack to the degree that she desired. For Jack, though finally pushed into a corner where he had to fight back to emotionally survive, his No was not an affirmation of some value that could be life defining. Without a clear sense of self-worth, he could never be the person his wife desired him to be. It is a sad story that is not unique based on the conversations that I have had with people over the years.

We all say yes to requests. Some of these requests are fair and valid. Others are not. Our problem is that if we say yes to them all, we lose touch with what matters to us. This is what Jean described to me during our work session.

> Me: How much time during the course of the day would be saved if this relation between yes and no was healthy? Any idea?

> Jean: It's not how many hours during the day, it's years. I don't think you can equate it in a day because, over time, days to moms and women don't exist. It's like, *the days are long, the years are short.* Right? That's what you always hear. …

> So every day you're thinking, what have I done today? You've said yes to lunch. You said yes to that person … yes to PTA. …

> I don't think hours in the day exist for women because unless you are someone who has every minute planned and is okay with the control that you lose when your child gets sick or whatever, then those days run into each other. So, our sense of purpose over

time is affected for sure. … I talk to people all the time who say, I volunteered for this, I'm on the committee for my child's fundraiser. All these fundraisers that everyone's doing... Do we need to do the fundraiser? Just write a check or don't... And it's all about the auctions and this stuff, and it gets ... the pressures … the social pressures. … as a mother, as a working mom, it's hard to manage. … They've had it with their husband, or they're exhausted by their children. They've had it with their husband because he hasn't played a role in these daily decisions of saying yes and no. Right? Men have their purpose. Women have a purpose too, but it's different.

"The days are long, the years are short". A simple statement by Gretchen Rubin, author of The Happiness Project, said that "of everything that I've ever written … seems to resonate most deeply with people." It is a saying that has gone viral because it explains what people experience.

You can see in Jean's description of her experience how Mary may also feel the same way. Why do we say Yes, when we really want to say No? Why do we do this?

Somewhere in the subtle recesses of our mind, we may believe that we must say yes in order to preserve a relationship or ensure the success of a project. Many people have told me this. Like Jack, we go along to get along. We go over and above what is asked because we feel an obligation to contribute at a level no one else shares. Do we really believe that the success or survivability of a relationship or project is all on our shoulders? Why do we think this?

This doesn't just happen on a person-to-person level. It also happens on a grand social one. Magnify the obligation to say Yes from one person to ten or fifty, and it isn't about preserving a relationship, but our social standing. Magnify this perspective to how we fit into a social media world, and we get a global society captured by social fear of not fitting in.

Do you go along to get along? Do you try not to make a fuss or cause a disturbance? Or do you think about what is asked of you? Is there a line you will not cross? If we always say yes, then we may have lost touch with ourselves. We have become subjects of other people's opinions and the social pressures that follow. We are much more easily manipulated to always say Yes when we have lost perspective on what we value most.

What then does it take to say No? Is Jack standing up for himself a courageous beginning point?

I don't believe it is. It is an act of desperation. It is essentially a defensive action. I'm going to resist so that I don't totally lose my identity. Is the answer to Mary's determination to change Jack to simply isolate yourself emotionally from her by saying No to everything now?

Is Mary's standing up for her family a courageous act of a loving wife and mother? Or is it also an act of desperation, a defensive action to avoid having to change herself? Is Jack's half- measures of change only making her more determined to fix him?

What is missing that Jack and Mary need if they were to have any hope of resolving the differences that were driving them apart?

They need self-awareness. Now, it does take courage to become aware of who we are in real terms. In some sense, it feels easy to just be like everyone else. To go along to get along. It feels right to stand your ground as the lone defender of my family against a world of compromise.

Yet, what is the aim here? Is it to win? To beat your antagonist? Where is the Yes that gives reason for hope and reconciliation?

Every decision we make, large or small, affects us. Ever said Yes to something that clearly went against your principles? We feel grief and regret from it. We pledge to not do that again. We feel torn. We may say to ourselves, "Why didn't I see that coming?" As a result, we beat ourselves up over saying Yes to something when we clearly should have said No.

Maybe you invested some money in a friend's company or a vacation property that in retrospect doesn't make sense. In retrospect, we see how we compromised our life or our family's welfare so that now we suffer the consequences. We've all found ourselves in similar situations.

We may say Yes because we want to believe other people's intentions are always good and noble. We make these decisions because we are not clear about what is important. Our self- awareness of what we truly value is lacking. We are unable to think clearly because we are captivated by what other people think.

The only way to truly know how to say Yes or No is to test the assumption. In other words, you need to make your own decision. Do your own homework. Make up your own mind. Don't let yourself excuse it because you don't have time. You have all the time in the world for what is important.

Self-awareness is the first step towards self-understanding. Without self-understanding, we lose the capacity to distinguish between right and wrong. It has been said that all it takes for evil to succeed is for good people to do nothing. It can also be said that all it takes for evil to succeed is for people to say yes because they have no real reason not to do so.

Self-understanding isn't first understanding myself in relation to others. Rather, it is understanding what my values are. Then I have a basis for understanding what my relationships with people and the whole of my life should be. Values are the bedrock of our lives, the foundation upon every other part of our lives is built.

The core problem in Jack and Mary's marriage is that they have no core values that they shared mutually. They each saw marriage as a kind of utility that provides a context for the fulfillment of what they individually want in life. The problem was that both had learned how to be married from watching their parents and grandparents. Once the way of being married no longer satisfied them, the marriage was over. They never understood why they should be married. It was a social expectation that they had learned and never given much thought to its value and purpose.

What then do you believe about your life? To know this begins to define who you are. I am saying you need to know who you are that is not simply a reason acquired from your family and friends. For they are in the same situation. They seek to make you and others over into their own image because they are also looking for some affirmation.

If we peel back another layer of Jack and Mary's marriage, we'd find that they were looking for someone to marry who would fulfill some perceived lack in their life. Maybe that lack was their own insecurity or lack of a clear sense of identity. Or maybe, they married the person who they perceived as a replacement for the kind of father or mother that they wanted or needed growing up but did not have. The psychological dimensions of their choices are complex. As a result, they needed an external reference point that could provide them a place to go to be able to talk about these deep conflicts that each had within themselves.

One external reference point is our values. Our values are not only foundational. Once identified they need to be non-negotiable in order for these values to be allowed to fulfill their potential. We must be clear about what we value. When we say No, we are doing so because our values have pointed us towards the life that we choose, rather than the one we end up with.

Another external reference point for them could have been a trusted counselor. If the family exists solely as a social utility for each of the partners, then intimacy based upon a shared purpose is probably missing. Without a mutual commitment to shared values, it is difficult to create an environment where children may be loved and nurtured. The first step is the willingness to change.

Why We Don't Say No

The idea of making every No decision a Yes resonates deeply with people. You can see it in Jean's response. You can say No because you are really saying Yes to something else. This is not just a need that women have, but every man does also. We both need to be able to distinguish between what is important and essential in our lives and what is not.

Look behind the words of my conversation with Jean above, there is a truth that many of us do not want to face. It is the reality that many of our decisions are made to be amenable to others. Social conformity has a powerful hold on us. It means that much of our lives are lived complying with the expectations of others. While this is true for both men and women, I believe that women live with a greater burden because of their focus on relationships. This is why saying "Let every No be a Yes'" resonates so deeply with them.

We live every day in relationships with our children, spouse, co-workers, friends, and neighbors. The real impact of our lives happens in our interaction with people. I am convinced that we will be remembered after we die by our relationships with people. It will be our legacy. We must understand the kind of person we want to be in our relationships. If we are always conforming to other people's expectations, we easily could be seen as weak or unworthy of respect.

Our problem is not simply "Who am I?" It is the deeper question of how I can function as an individual in a world that makes demands upon me. Social conformity is a challenge that we must manage each day. I've been told by many women that they feel their lives are pulled in every direction because of their sense of responsibility. Do they have a greater sense of responsibility than men? I don't believe so. The difference is in understanding I am responsible for what and to whom?

Social conformity becomes tyrannical when we don't know how to say No. We don't know how because we don't know ourselves well enough. If we are unsure about who we are, how can we ever be in a relationship where respect, trust, and mutual accountability are the outcomes.

Because in those relationships, we can say No and be understood and affirmed.

On the other side of the question, if the pressure to socially conform did not bring some real benefits then I doubt we'd be talking about it right now. Social conformity is not a bad thing. It is a mixture of good and bad. What we need to learn is how to distinguish the good from the bad so that our No's can be a Yes. In other words, we are making choices about the people and places where we freely decide to conform to their expectations, and where we choose not to by saying No.

I've known many women who have resisted, shall we call it, domestic social conformity. They wanted something different. They wanted a career. They chose not to marry or to have children. Many women chose this path intentionally, and others find themselves there after a lifetime of choices. For those of us who did marry and have children, we need to see that their choice is not second best compared to ours, but rather their choice. We should recognize that whether a woman embraces a domestic life or a professional career, both paths come with social expectations. Many choose both and face the demands of meeting the social obligations of both worlds. It was my conversation with Jean, who is a businesswoman, wife, and mother that instigated the purpose of writing this book.

I am not sitting in judgment because a person chooses one path and not another. Rather, I aim to understand as objectively as possible the realities that our personal and social choices demand of us. To do so I hope to provide insight, or rather, a way to approach these questions so that we may find our lives to be better.

In this context, I see how confusing these demands upon us can be. It makes it difficult to say No when we must weigh the relative merits of a decision against the competing demands of all the social settings we live and work in.

Chapter Two:
Why Is It Hard To Say No?

We must learn to say No. I'm not talking about a toddler who screams No because he doesn't want to do something. Instead, I'm focusing on saying No as an expression of our unique individuality. We are not just saying No to others. We are also saying No to ourselves.

We learn by imitation. It is not just imitation by example, but imitation by appropriating the desire of the person we are imitating. Historian Rene' Girard unearthed this insight into human nature. Here is a portion of an interview that Girard had with David Cayley of the CBC.

> Desire is essentially borrowed desire. There is no such thing as natural desire, otherwise it would be instinct. If desire had a fixed object, it couldn't change, and it would be the same thing as

animal instinct. Therefore, desire comes always from the other. Therefore, this other, if he is close enough socially or physically, will necessarily become our rival when we desire his object.

In close social settings, even online, imitation is a part of conforming to the social expectations of the group. The more our imitation of the expectations of the group grows, the more we want what they want or they have, the closer we come to one another.

In the story of Jack and Mary, the closer they became as husband and wife in physical proximity to one another, the more in conflict they became. Girard points this out.

> The marvelous paradox is that the closer you are, the more your goals will be the same. And this will be true at the highest level, at the intellectual level. If we are really close intellectually, we're going to look for the same things. And there will be moments when we will feel that the other is more successful than we are. As a matter of fact, it's everybody's tendency to feel that the other is more successful. It's also everybody's tendency to feel I am more successful, or I should be more successful.

But anyway, the problem will be there because Man is essentially a dynamic individual, who wants to occupy the whole ground. And this individualism will lead us into competition with the people who are closest to us.

Ironically, Jack and Mary had the same goals. They both wanted a family. However, they wanted it for different reasons. Once their marriage became a family with children, it became a source of conflict. Each person had their own way of controlling their spouse. Jack wanted his career with the family as a slightly secondary responsibility. Mary wanted her whole life, including her life with Jack, totally immersed in the family. This is where their real conflict emerged.

Think of the comment section of blogs or Facebook or Instagram posts. Here we have a group of people who are close in belief and adherence to the social expectations of the group. What then happens? Competition grows between people. Criticism, condescension, trolling, and ultimately, canceling emerge as the group's behaviors. At some point, social violence erupts as people are ostracized or kicked out of the group. This behavior is not limited to social media groups. We see it in businesses, schools, and politics.

Rene Girard wrote extensively on this mimetic desire of imitation leading to violence. He is best known for describing The Scapegoat phenomenon. As competition within a group or organization grows, conflict and violence develop. The mechanism for addressing this crisis is to identify someone to blame. They become the scapegoat, the sacrificial lamb, the one who must be discarded in order to bring peace back to the group.

In Jack and Mary's case, Jack became Mary's scapegoat. He had to be sacrificed to preserve the sanctity of her belief in the family unit. Once Jack is gone, peace in the family is restored. Is she happy? Now, that is a different question. Because what brings peace is quite often the internalization of conflict as self-righteousness, which is rarely a happy place to be.

In my own assessment of Girard's thought, the human problem is that we don't know ourselves. We look to other people to define us. This is why it is so easy to simply conform.

We've already cast our lot with the group. We may as well go along to remain in good standing. This is precisely what happened in Germany in the 1930s as the National Socialists under Adolph Hitler came to power. After the war, during the Nuremburg war trials, Nazi officers were asked why they committed the atrocities that they did. Their answer? "We were following orders."

So, it is today. We follow orders because we desire to be a part of the group, to join, to conform to the expectations of those we seek to imitate.

The problem that we must address if we are going to be able to say No is to have a better understanding of what it means to be our own person within the social structures of the world we live and work in.

Two Sides to the Social Coin

A problem that we all face is that we don't just live a social life in relationships with others. We also live an individual life. The conflict at the heart of our decisions is where these two parts of our lives come together. Imagine our lives as a coin with two sides representing our individual selves and our social selves.

The conversations that prompted this book are about that point of connection between the two parts of our lives. It is a question about how can we be ourselves as individuals and at the same time be participants in a wider social world. It is not easy because the effect of online culture is to prescribe who we must be in order to find acceptance. The pressure to socially conform means that there will always be a conflict between our individual selves and the social world. How do we live an authentic life as an individual person who is also living in a diverse and complex social world?

Giving and Taking

One way to describe this story is as a tension between *giving* and *taking*. The individual side of our life *takes* to feed its physical, emotional, intellectual, and spiritual parts. It is born in the drive for advancement and preservation. If we don't *take* care of ourselves, we will live a sad and dissipated life.

On the other hand, there is the *giving* side of our lives. It is a place where we sacrifice for the good of our family, our community, and our nation. The *giving* side seeks to make the world a better place. Fulfillment in life comes from *giving*, not *taking*. Yet, if we do not provide for ourselves, ultimately, we will be empty, with nothing left to *give*. This tension requires balance. A balance that is never fixed, always evolving.

This simple perspective can clarify our own motivations for *taking* and *giving*. A lifetime involvement in community and philanthropic projects has shown me that people's reasons for *giving* and *taking* are not always easily discerned. In many respects, the giving of wealth is a path to increased wealth. Our *giving* and *taking* need to be accountable to the values that we have chosen to define our lives.

Is Balance the Answer?

Can you see how the two sides to the coin represent who we are in a simple, yet complete sense? On one side there is the unique person that I am. On the flip side, there is the person who takes on many different roles based upon the social context of the situation.

To be a whole person, we need a strong sense of self, of who we are, and what the meaning of life is for us. We need to be able to distinguish ourselves from the crowd. Just as we seek to imitate those we wish to be like. We should also choose not to imitate those we believe are not worth following. There is a choice here. A choice that is constantly being made as we interact with people. This is how we find the strength to say No or I disagree.

We also need a healthy social environment. Think of this social structure as an organization. It has a purpose, a set of rules that people are expected to follow, and an identifiable leadership structure. It is more like a culture than an organization. Being a social structure, it is organized through relationships. A healthy one will be aware of the dangers of competition to control.

Look at the social environment of your social media platforms. Some of the people that you interact with may be people you know from other places. Maybe you went to the same school or you work together, or your kids are on the same sports team. Our direct relationships come from the variety of these settings.

How do we measure the quality of these relationships? It isn't easy to describe what a quality relationship is. Especially if our principal relationships are online. What do we expect from our connections on Instagram, Twitter, or Facebook? Just a Like check? Maybe a comment? How about on YouTube? Is it to subscribe or to send a Patreon donation? How are these connections real relationships? More specifically, what are the values that represent our online relationships?

This is part of the reason why relationships are hard to measure. The context is constantly changing. An indication that we are always in transition. Anyone who has been married understands that the relationship changes over time. Our measure of its quality must include principles that are suited to this specific moment in time. Also, there are those qualities that transcend time.

Let us call those qualities values. The most difficult to maintain may well be the ones that are most worth preserving. I am referring to *respect, trust, and mutual accountability*. Do we not expect this from all of our relationships whether they are direct ones or mere connections through social media? We may find that many of our relationships or connections lack mutual respect. Instead, we have the pressure to conform. It is for this reason that we need not only to be clear about who we are as individuals, but how we want our social relationships to be.

Our identity is one side of the coin. The other side of the coin is our relationships and social connections. Diminish one or the other of the two sides of the coin, and our sense of well-being and how we function in the world suffers. Our lives become out of balance, even broken. We first feel it. At some critical stage, we begin to look for solutions. It is this search that has brought people to me. It is also one of the reasons I am writing this book.

The two sides of this coin are not equal. One side is always dominant. But not dominant all the time. Each one vies for our attention. The healthy person, over time, figures out how to find the right balance between the two sides. Our difficulty is that balance is never fixed. It is a moving target. Every day we need to focus on both sides of the coin.

A balance between the two sides of the coin, while a worthy goal, is almost impossible to achieve. It sounds too much like equal emphasis. As Girard might describe it, when things are equal there is competition, possibly violence. This explains to me why in my country where equality has been greater than any in human history, there is so much violence. It is that mimetic desire to own the whole which makes equality an elusive goal to ultimately achieve.

The conflict in the engagement between our individual and social selves. This is what Jean was pointing us towards. Being an individual and taking care of oneself physically, mentally, emotionally, and spiritually requires a different kind of effort than participating and contributing to a social environment. Both sides make demands upon us. The difficulty of achieving balance is that *giving* or *taking* often diminishes the other, instead of strengthening the whole. The more we *give*, the less we focus on our needs. The more I *take* to meet "my" needs, the less my life matters to others. This is the problem that I see in the idea of balance. We need a way of approaching these two parts of our lives.

The difficulty we face in creating balance is that we are always confronted by choices between the individual and the social. We become caught in a binary trap between the two sides.

Balance is impossible because we are always choosing between one or the other. It is either/or. Yet, I believe that we can solve this problem by approaching our lives as a whole seeking alignment and integrity.

The problem with the binary trap of trying to balance *giving* and *taking* is that we are forced into a position where we see our social life in antagonism to our personal life. It may well be an accurate picture of our lives. Look back at Jean's conversation with me. She longs to be able to say No. Why? Because she feels an obligation to conform to the expectations that the people in her social circles of family, friends, and work have for her. The solution is not to reject those social expectations in favor of being independent and self-sufficient. Nor is it to give in to the pressure of social conformity. As I have suggested, it isn't in trying to balance the two sides either.

The Alignment Alternative

As a person who has lived a long life at the intersection of the individual and the social, I still live with the conflict of the two sides of this coin. Each of the facets of our lives represents something we value. They have a claim upon us. A claim upon our time, our resources, and our personal commitments. The more we look at the full breadth of our lives, the two-sided coin looks too simplistic. Instead, our lives are more like a large, hundred-sided die. Toss the die to see who gets a piece of us today. Of course, our priorities are not set by random chance. Rather, it is more like which one screams the loudest. It is a poor way to live our lives. Yet, this is what many of us do. The result being we are being drained dry as we say Yes to everything that claims our attention.

Instead of trying to balance all the competing demands upon our lives, I believe that focusing on alignment is a better path for us. Alignment is a way of creating order by being clear about what we value. What we value is defined by our values. These ideas best express the kind of person we want to be and the life we want to have.

It is important to be clear about what I mean by values. Most of us who have families value them. We accept the responsibilities and complexity of it. In Jack and Mary's situation, they both valued family. But they didn't value it in the same way. That difference is also a difference in value.

Canadian philosopher Charles Taylor helps us here by making a particular distinction about two orders of desire. Jack and Mary both desire to be married, to have children, and to be a family. This is what Taylor might call a first-order desire. We can see this as the family having a utilitarian value for both Jack and Mary. The family is a means to an end which satisfies a desire that they share. They both believe in the family. Yet, they believe in its value differently.

The second-order desire is where Jack and Mary's conflict emerges. Jack liked the idea of being married. It was a social good for him. Until Mary's attitude towards him changed, he was happy with the arrangement. He had rather low expectations for marriage and family life. As long as there were not too many conflicts, he liked being married. Mary, on the other hand, saw family as an ultimate value for her. The family was an expression of her personal identity. Her expectations were high for every aspect of it. The difference between Jack and Mary reflect different second-order desires by each of them, even though they shared a first-order desire of belief in the family.

Another way to understand this distinction is to see that first-order desires are primarily about what we individually want. We desire to have our hunger satisfied each day. We want to eat when we want to eat regardless of how it may impact anyone else. Second-order desires are rooted in the decisions that we make in relationship with other people, like our family or our co-workers. We learn to discern the choices of other people, and we accommodate to their preferences, and they to ours. Second-order desires are the basis for making decisions in society. At the heart of those desires are our values.

When we say No that is a Yes, we are making a second-order decision. We are making a choice. We are saying this activity that everyone else wants to do, I will not do because I find it will compromise a value that is important to me. This is how a No becomes a Yes.

I could give you a list of values as your second order reasons to say Yes or No. But those would be my values, not yours. It is important that we each discover the values that provide the basis for our decision and choices in life.

If you were like Jack, a go-along-to-get-along kind of person, then you would be adopting values that only matter for fitting into a social situation. To do that would miss an essential element of the process of alignment. Our values are discovered through experience and reflection. Think of it as a distillation process. We cook off the ideas, the notions, the assumptions or the ideologies that are not essential, leaving the pure, distilled liquid of meaning to drink from every day.

In another book in this series, I wrote about how honor became the principal value that defines my life. I didn't arrive at that idea by going down a list and picking it. Instead, I experienced being honored by a stranger in a far-away land, whom I did not know by name, with whom I could not communicate in his language, and never saw again after our moment of encounter. His honor towards me was one of gratitude, of thanks for contributing to his people. It was a moment of transformation for me. I had never been treated with honor and deep gratitude.

The experience has defined life. It has helped me to make sense of other situations where values like respect, trust, generosity, and acceptance are practiced.

Alignment is different from balance in this way. Instead of seeing the two sides of the coin like a child's see-saw, each side rising and falling in importance, there is a third side to the coin. The edge is value, purpose, meaning, and self-knowledge which brings the two sides together as one coin. Instead of two sides at either end of a straight line, there are the two faces of the coin joined together by the values that define us. This third side, our values, pulls both our individualism and our social environment towards it. The closer the two sides are the less the two sides struggle for individual dominance.

When we are confident in knowing what matters to us, and consequently what doesn't matter, we can find a way to say No that affirms a value or stated purpose or a relationship that matters to us. In doing so, we are making a No a Yes. While we can see how this is where we want to be, this doesn't solve the problem of the conflict that exists between our individuality and the pressure of social conformity. In Chapter Three, we will apply my Circle of Impact model to our problem - It is OUR problem, yours and mine – to find a solution that best fits our situation.

Part Three:
Solving the Problem of No

The problem of making our No's a Yes is not learning how to say No. It is rather knowing our own mind, being clear about our own values, and being able to translate those ideas into ways of life that build strength in our relationships, our families, and in the work that we do. Saying No is just a way to frame the importance of these aspects of our lives.

It is one thing to know that we need to say No, it is another thing to do it. Even though we know that we need to base our No's on the affirmation of some value or values, there is still a gap between knowing and accomplishing. In this chapter, I want to show you how we can achieve this through the alignment that is possible in the Circle of Impact model.

Understanding Where To Begin

Let's define what we want to achieve?

We could say, "I want to say No more." This would echo Jean's thoughts above. Is that really what we want? Just to be able to say No?

Why is that important?

In the previous chapter I introduced the concept from Charles Taylor that as human beings we have two orders of desire. Being able to say No is a basic or first order of desire. We desire to be free of the obligations to say Yes, when we really want to say No.

We are able to do that because we have discovered a second order of desire. If we think of order as assigning value to the many aspects of our lives, some will rank higher than others. Second order decisions are ones where we evaluate and decide what is important. Those decisions are based on criteria that are important to us. The most powerful, life-defining ones are our values.

This means that if we want to get to the place where we are free to say No and Yes in an authentic way, we need to know what our values are. As I said above, we tend to discover these values as we live. Therefore, let us frame our question in terms of clarifying the values that are important to us.

What are the values that I want to define my life?

If we can identify them, then I believe the path to alignment will be clear. And all your No's can be a Yes.

Values That Matter

We could spend all day talking about values and find that we are trying to find the perfect value. To do so just complicates our lives. The values that we need provide clarity of purpose and simplicity of application. As a result, I would like to begin looking at values by asking a simple question.

What do you want to change?

If you could change anything in the world, what would it be? Would it be something social, personal, something having to do with the past, or with the future?

You are going to change something. You either do so by saying No or Yes. You do so by doing nothing or doing something. Every decision leads to some change. I would like you to see that by identifying the values that are important to you that then you take initiative to change what you truly want to change. By being intentional, we affirm our own agency as a person. As you learn to take initiative, you increasingly become your own person, knowing you own mind, and able to with confidence and logic say No because it affirms the Yes of your values. This is what Jean is pointing towards. She wants to change how she lives in the context of her work and family.

So, what do you want to change?

Hiding in the shadows behind this question is some experience that points in the opposite direction. It is the experience that you don't want to repeat. It is the No that becomes a Yes.

I've had a number of people speak to me about the ugliness that appears in social media interaction. It is something that they would like to see changed. They try by not returning hate for hate. In that instance you changed yourself. Maybe that isn't enough. Maybe this change means walking away altogether.

What is it that matters to people that makes them want to change the culture of social media? They tell me they want to see respect between people. Respect is a value. To change respect in society requires us to begin to treat ourselves with self-respect. For many people this means beginning to say No. They refuse to engage in the kind of negativity that bothers them.

Long lasting, real change is a grassroots, bottom-up process. It begins within us and grows out to our relationships, then the society around us.

Let's see how we can begin to elevate respect as a life-defining value in your life.

Begin with a list of people, places, and organizations where you are regularly involved. It could be work, your children's school and their activities, your place of worship, or a shop where you are a loyal customer.

Now, ask, do they respect me as a friend, colleague, or customer? What kind of behaviors should I expect if they respect me? Did I see them one time or often? I am asking for you to look for patterns. Behaviors that repeat themselves. If you can identify the behaviors that show you respect, then you can do those, repeating them often with people, and you develop a healthy set of behavior patterns that people will begin to associate with you.

Based on what respect means to you, do you see two lists forming? There is a list of those who respect you, and one for those who don't? At this point, are we beginning to see how a value, like respect, begins to matter in how we view the circumstances of our lives. When a value, like respect, becomes a measuring tool for situations, we can begin to take the next step and say, "I'm not going to participate in that project because it is not clear that my contribution has their respect." This lack of respect may have nothing to do with you personally. It may be how the group looks at those whom they serve or ask for financial support.

The turning point in Jack and Mary's marriage was the moment each realized that their spouse no longer respected them. What a tragic moment that is when you realize that this person that you fell in love with, committed your life to, now, no longer respects you.

If respect has been lost, then it is most likely true that other similar values have lost their defining value. The loss of respect in Jack and Mary's relationship would also include a loss of belief in emotional transparency and physical intimacy. How can you place yourself in a trusting, vulnerable position with someone you no longer respect?

Values matter because they define how we act in our relationships. They don't just define our identity. They guide how we live.

Let's look at a different scenario. Nick grew up in a broken and abusive home and came to believe that the world is made up of victims and victimizers. He believes that victims lack the discipline to control their life circumstances. Two paths are presented to Nick, both having discipline as the core value that defines his life. One path is that of gang member of a criminal enterprise. The other is as a member of the military. Both paths require discipline. The question that Nick faces is also one of respect.

The abuse he received from his father was always about respecting him out of fear. He knew enough that he did not want to become his father. Eventually, Nick was removed from his home and placed into the foster care system. It was there Nick saw the opposite of the victimizer. What is a person who is neither a victim nor a victimizer? This is all Nick knew. His foster parent was a US Army Staff Sergeant. He was a disciplined, no-nonsense man. He was also fair and attentive to the behavioral challenges that Nick brought to the family. Nick's childhood robbed him of the ability to stand on his own and be self-sufficient. He needed

structure as the ground for his discipline. As a result, through his foster father's care, Nick finished high school, and enlisted in the military.

Discipline and order were values that Nick longed to be a part of his life. All he had known until he went to live with his foster family was chaos and violence. Nick was an ideal candidate to join a criminal street gang. There he would find structure and order. It would have been the order of a victim becoming a victimizer. Yet, a different kind of man intervened and showed him a different path to achieve discipline and order in his life.

Values are not just ideas, but ways of seeing how we want our lives to be. In the Circle of Impact, values are part of the Ideas dimension. They help us to define our purpose for impact, and the kind of relationships that are healthy. The values that define you and are central to your relationships are ones that matter within the context of your life. They are not simply good ideas. They are ideas that provide a basis for letting your No be a Yes.

Creating the Alignment that Matters

Let's return to this idea of alignment, rather than balance. Alignment brings the three dimensions of the Circle of Impact together. This approach places impact as the focal point for alignment. In the moment where we need to decide Yes or No, we need to ask a few simple questions.

What is the desired impact that I want from this choice that I have to make?

By this, we mean, what changes if I say Yes or No? Are we clear about this desired change?

What happens to my values when I say Yes or No to this choice? Are my values elevated or diminished by choice?

Am I compromising my values by saying Yes? How do I know which is the best choice?

It only takes but a few minutes to ask these questions. We ask because they enter us into a decision-making process. When you are clear about your values. And you understand the connection of your values to your choices of No and Yes. Then you can make better decisions for yourself, your family, and for business and community.

In my conversation with Jean, she speaks about the fundraisers that she is asked to participate in and contribute to at her childrens' school. It is clear that she would like to say No. If she was to ask the above questions quickly in the moment of choosing, she would see the outcome or impact of the choice emerging out of the fog of uncertainty.

What these questions reveal in Jean's situation is that it is not enough just to have some set of values. We also need a clear sense of purpose that is derived from those values.

What then is the purpose of these fundraisers? Is it to raise money? Or, is it a higher purpose which is to build parental commitment to the school and its programs? If it is the latter reason, we should then ask, are these campaigns actually structured to build stronger support for the school?

Purpose here leads back to our relationships. Are these programs creating a culture of support that transcends who is in charge, what the program is, and how to create a deeper level of commitment than previously seen?

Our values and purpose for impact become aligned with our relationships and the structure of the situation where we are involved. Is Jean's frustration pointing to a lack of alignment that is represented by what I call "a persistent, residual culture of relationships?" This is a culture of values that persists because it resides in the relationships of the people involved. Do the fundraising campaigns at Jean's kids school need to focus on creating an alignment which creates this kind of culture of support? Probably so.

We are not just thinking people, or relating people, or people who live and work within some kind of social or organizational structure. We are people for whom all these aspects of our lives operate cooperatively. When they do, our capacity to see the No that is a Yes grows.

Part Four:
Five Questions for
Getting to Yes

Why and How to Ask Questions

To gain clarity about our situations so that our No's can be a Yes, we need to ask questions. I've already had you asking questions through the course of this book. Now, I want to provide a simple set of five questions that you can use in any situation to gain clarity, align your life, and stay on track towards the goals that you have. I call them The Five Questions that Everyone Must Ask. I believe you can ask them in relation to every situation or aspect of your life.

If Jack and Mary had begun early enough in their marriage to ask these questions about their marriage and their family, two changes would have occurred. The first is that they would have transitioned from being two independent individuals to living as husband and wife. They would also have discovered the source of the problem areas that lay hidden for years. These questions are worth asking because they allow us to ask the hard questions about our own responsibilities for the challenges that we face.

When I introduce these questions to people, I tell them that the first time that they go through them to take only 5-10 minutes. Quickly write a word or phrase down. Just get an initial familiarity with the questions. Then the next time, take a longer time. Eventually, these questions will always been present in your mind when you having to make a decision that does not initially have a clear answer.

The Five Questions are ...

1. What has changed? How am I in transition?

2. What is my impact?

3. Who am I impacting?

4. What opportunities do I have because of the impact that I am having?

5. What problems have I created? What obstacles do I face?

Begin by identifying the situation you want to address. It could be a major decision, meeting planning, or analyzing a problem that has arisen in the family. You can use the questions to look back, to prepare for the present moment, and to look forward. The beauty of these questions is that they have a universal application. Here's an example.

Dawn and Dan's Path To Yes

Dawn and Dan have a busy family life. Both have their own businesses that provide them flexibility for their family commitments. They have four children. Two girls and two boys. Stacy, the oldest, plays soccer. Sandy is into choir and cheer team. The boys, Danny and Doug, are twins and they do everything together. They play sports at school and are in scouts.

The situation that sparked the need to ask the Five Questions was Stacy, the oldest, being invited to join a traveling soccer team. Dawn and Dan realized that they had to give their full commitment to this opportunity for Stacy. They understood that this was a step towards her earning a college athletic scholarship.

How do you support each child fairly when they are at different ages and stages of development? How do you manage two businesses with four kids when almost every week there is travel involving one of your children? Who are you going to say No to in the family?

The precise problem that Dawn and Dan had to resolve was two-fold? How do they create a schedule for the family that was fair to each child? But not just fair to each child, how do they identify and plan for the opportunities of growth and development for each child? Instead of trying to avoid playing favorites, how to treat each child as a favorite in their own way?

As a father of three children, we faced this dilemma. Even though they are each grown and married, I face this dilemma. For you love your children. But you don't love them the same way. This is the challenge and Dawn and Dan faced with Stacy's opportunity.

Dawn and Dan also faced the dilemma how to operate their two businesses while taking care of each child. Imagine the stress they felt on a daily basis. Imagine the demands on the marriage relationship in an environment where, in many ways, each parent must deny themselves in order to be at their best for their kids. This is not an exceptional story. This is a normal story that families face today.

They begin with the first question.

What has changed? How are we in transition?

Stacy's opportunity to join the traveling soccer squad is the initial signal that there is a challenging situation at hand. Dawn and Dan's children have aged into a time of high activity in school and after-school. Greater demands for attention to each child's development during the critical middle and high school years also presses in on them. There is a feeling present that they have to get this right because they won't get another opportunity. Of course, that really isn't true, but in this moment, this is what they feel.

In addition, there is already less time for Dawn and Dan as a couple. They anticipate that this period of time will last for approximately five to seven years. For Stacy, the oldest, is a sophomore in high school and Sandy is a freshman. The boys are in 7th grade.

What has changed? The dynamics of the family where the four children once were treated as single unit. Load them in the car. Go to the store. Visit grandparents. Come home. Now each child has their own schedule and development plan.

What is our impact?

The impact question is about the change identified above. What is the impact on the family? Obviously they are busier. But that is not the change that really matters in this instance. Rather, what is the effect of this point in time on each member of the family?

What is the impact on Stacy as she travels with the soccer team? Is it greater confidence and stronger skills? Is it greater clarity about just how much she wants to play soccer in college? This is the conversation that Dawn and Dan can be having with her as she goes through her own season of transition.

Sandy has a different personality than Stacy. She is not driven to achieve like Stacy. Instead she loves being on the cheer team with her friends and singing. She is the most extroverted of the four kids. She likes the excitement of the performance. She loves games and is the child who is the social glue that holds the family together as she gets the family to play games together. Her favorite is Charades.

The boys, Danny and Doug, are happy playing sports and going on a camping trips with scouts once a month. Dan is an assistant with the scout troop and attends the weekly meetings with the boys. It is their time together as guys. The boys are just beginning to see the world as something to reach for. They are the most creative of the four kids. Danny is always drawing. Doug loves making up funny stories. They talk about creating their own comic book.

Dawn and Dan are asking the impact question from three points of view. What is the impact they want for each child? What is the impact that we want for us as a family? What is the impact of our family upon our businesses? Presently, Dawn's office is at home. Dan's business is in an office park 15 minutes away.

This question has brought clarity to their situation. Not just clarity in a general sense that they see a problem. They now have a clearer focus on what is the goal for each child, the family, and their businesses. They define the impact by the pathway to it.

- For Stacy, it is preparation for college.

- For Sandy, it is music and voice lessons.

- For Danny, it is taking drawing classes at the local arts center.

- For Doug, it is enrollment in an online course in story writing.

- For Dawn and Dan, as a couple, it is an anniversary trip to Hawaii.

- For the Family, it is two hours on Sunday night as Family night for dinner, games or a movie.

- For Dawn's business, it is hiring an assistant to manage her schedule and communication with clients.

- For Dan, it is the reorganization of the office to allow him time to be available early mornings and after school.

In Dawn and Dan's family situation, the impact question is not about the past, but about how the present flows into the future. Every decision that they now make has consequences for the whole family for months and years to come. Gaining clarity about the impact that they want means freedom to live without fear or worry about where each child is going. As all plans should be, they know that this is now, and flexibility will be needed as life's unexpected transitions come at them.

Who is impacted?

This question looks beyond the individual, and in this case, beyond the family. The seven impact focal points that Dawn and Dan have identified each take place within a context of relationships. Asking these questions prepares them for moments when they are asked to take on additional responsibilities, whether with the kids' activities or within their business relationships. To some people they know their No will have to be strong and definitive. For others, they can say, maybe there's another way. Most importantly, for each person who supports their family are resources to fulfill the opportunities that come with the seven goals

The first set of relationships beyond the family impact are Dawn and Dan's parents. They need them for times when Dawn travels with Stacy to a tournament and Dan is camping with the boys. During those times, Sandy will stay with friends or her grandparents.

In many respects, those most impacted by this scenario are Dawn and Dan. They have to make all sorts accommodations to the schedules of their children. Their lives are far better aligned than Jack and Mary. They communicate constantly, daily coordinate the family's schedule, and collaborate on the planning and the organization of the family's life.

Beyond the family, there is an impact upon the people at school and in all the kid's activities. Dawn is in constant contact with Stacy's teachers to make sure she stays up-to-date on her school work. The hidden impact is in how each child's experience impacts their siblings. As schedules become more demanding, the four kids as a unit begin to separate into their own specific path of development. As a result, the kids talk about road trips to Stacy's games and fall football games with Sandy. The boys want to take the family camping to their favorite site.

The First Three Questions Impact

The first three questions provide a foundation of awareness. The questions are readily available to ask the clarifying questions that are needed in the moment of crisis or conflict.

Here's an example of a board meeting where Dan serves.

Sitting in a local non-profit board meeting hearing reports, Dan senses that something seems off. He can't pinpoint it. Quietly and quickly he asks.

When was this change first spoken about? Was it in this meeting or a previous one? Or, is this something discussed privately that the board is only now learning about?

Dan, then, speaks up.

"I have a couple of questions.

Why are we just now hearing about this change? It sounds like there has already been considerable conversation about it? When did this first come up? (Question One.)

What is the impact of the change that you are now asking us to endorse? (Question Two.)

Lastly, it is not clear to me who benefits from this change? (Question Three.)"

In a moment, Dan by asking the first three questions, has not only brought clarity to the discussion, but focused attention on who are the beneficiaries of the recommended action.

The first three questions move us from initial awareness to a depth of understanding quickly and clearly. It places our awareness into the context of time so that we can track changes leading to the moment that we are focused upon. Then we can plan for the transitions that need to be created for the future.

In the story of Dawn and Dan's family, we see that their clarity focuses specifically on a particular aspect of their children's development right now. With that clarity being captured in a schedule for each member, moments of conflict can be anticipated and addressed before happening.

In many respects, this story is an idealized account of a family. However, it is also true that such an organizational structure for a family is dependent on the relationship of Dawn and Dan being healthy. To ask the questions we need a context where communication is open, honest, respectful, and transparent. Can the question help a couple navigate from a more closed communication pattern to an open one? Yes, as long as each member is willing to accept the responsibility for change that is identified in the process.

What opportunities do we now have?

If we have done good work on the first three questions, then the process will open up ways to take advantage of what we've seen. An opportunity is simply an invitation to take action that either resolves some problem or provides us a way to create impact. Impact is a change that makes a difference that matters.

For Dawn and Dan, the process provided them a framework for understanding how to manage the competing demands of their children at a critical time in their lives.

Later as Stacy moved on to play college soccer, and Sandy began to sing in regional

competitions, Dawn and Dan met people who asked them, "How do you do it?" They were asked so many times, they created a seminar for families in similar situations.

Both Dawn and Dan say that the greatest opportunity that came from this process was to see their children gain awareness about the differences between their family and many of their friends. Danny and Doug, as they got older, found themselves mentoring younger scouts who did not have a father at home. While their creative sides never diminished, they began to see a purpose for their lives beyond it. By their junior year, the twins' ambitions had diverged. Danny sought admission to one of the national military academies, while Doug decided that he was not ready for college. His senior year he self-published his first book of short stories. He stayed at home, worked nights, and wrote during the day.

Opportunities emerge as each step in the process of asking questions is done and repeated.

What problems have we created?
What obstacles do we face?

It may seem that the story of Dawn and Dan and their family was made easy by just asking the questions. Yet, in order for their multiple goals to be met, it required significant change by them. It could be said that you don't know what you have until what you have is an obstacle to what you want. This was true for Dawn and Dan.

Both grew up in families where they were the oldest child. Life was simple because neither of their families were particularly ambitious. Dan's dad was a supervisor at a local manufacturer. He'd come home at night tired from the demands of dealing with people and their problems all day. He would enjoyed relaxing, watching whatever game was on the television. His mom was a teacher at his elementary school. Dawn's parents owned a local hardware store. Neither their parents nor the course of their childhood prepared Dawn and Dan for life with four children in a world where their children's development takes such a great priority.

Dan's parents were not particularly attentive to his developmental needs. Dawn on the other hand grew up working side-by-side with her parents in their little family hardware store. She learned how to run a business, how to interact with customers, how to merchandise the shelves, and so many other things. What she didn't learn was how to be a parent. She was more a co-worker to her parents. In this sense, both Dawn and Dan entered parenthood with an inadequate awareness of what children need. It was not the only obstacle they faced.

Right out of college, Dan advanced quickly in a sales position with the company that hired him. He was on the road four days a week. He was a natural at client work. He quickly made more money than his college friends. He and Dawn bought new cars, and then a house that was beyond their means. Just as they were starting to talk about having their first child, reality hit them hard. The structure of their lives was poorly aligned for them to be parents. They had created a significant problem where they were financially over-extended. In addition, Dan was never home.

It was a moment of transition for Dawn and Dan. They had to decide what they wanted from life together, rather than accepting what life gave them. They began to think in terms of the impact that they wanted to have with their lives. Dan could continue to climb through the ranks of the company, making more and more money, or he could quit and find a local job that didn't require him to travel. At this point, Dawn was unhappy in the two jobs that she had had since college. She realized that she really wanted to work for herself. They realized that before they could have a child they needed to resolve their financial difficulties. They sold the home and the cars. They downsized. Dan opened an insurance agency. Dawn studied to become a coach for women in management. Problems solved. Obstacles removed.

Question Five leads us to see that even clear plans for the future must address the problems and obstacles that stand in the way. Especially those that we are responsible for creating.

The reality that I have found in using the Five Questions myself, and seeing others use them as well, is that if we are unwilling to address the consequences of our actions, we will never see clearly enough the precise changes that need to be done to achieve our goals.

The Five Question In Summary

1. What has changed? How am I in transition?

2. What is my impact?

3. Who am I impacting?

4. What opportunities do I have because of the impact that I am having?

5. What problems have I created? What obstacles do I face?

These questions are a vital tool for clarifying perspective in the moment of need. Ask these questions at least weekly and you'll begin to think deliberately about what is before you. You'll cease to be reactive, instead you'll respond from a position of strength.

The Five Questions help you to see:

- The transitions that we experience through changing circumstances.

- The change we can create that makes a difference that matters.

- The people who are a part of whatever situation is before you right now.

- The opportunities that await your initiative.

- The problems and obstacles that must be resolved if your desire impact is to be fulfilled.

Use the Five Questions when you need clarity about your values and purpose. Ask the questions when you are planning a meeting, a project, a family trip or life after children. The Five Questions is the surest path to be able to say No that is a Yes.

Chapter Five:
May All Your No's Be Yes'

Who Am I?

We may all ask this personal question in quiet moments of reflection or in times of deep moral conflict. It is a question deeply philosophical at its core. It is also the most practical of all questions. Who am I in the practice of my life?

Most of us don't have the luxury of time to sit and ponder these questions. Yet, we seek perspective by looking at videos, reading books, and listening to podcasts. We are constantly searching for meaning and insight into who we are. More so as our world has entered a time of great transition.

The ancients admonished us to "Know Thyself!" Yet how do we do this when the marketplace of ideas is so pressurized by social expectations to conform. How can a person stand on their own, knowing who they truly are in the midst of a world where social isolation and humiliation are the penalties for non-conformity? This is the macro-landscape of personal identity.

The micro-landscape is the one where every decision is a reflection of whether I choose to conform to social obligations or I make my decisions based upon the values that I have chosen to define who I am.

Think about the situation that we find ourselves in today. There are now two coins in our pocket. One coin we've already considered where the personal and the social are two sides of one coin. The other coin is similar. We find here the philosophical and practical parts of our life. These two coins represent four ways we are pulled in our lives.

We can be more philosophical than practical. Choose to live in our heads with our philosophy of life to guard us against the harshness of the world. When we treat ideas as a defense against the hard things of life, we may find ourselves blind to other ways that may also provide answers for us.

Or we can choose not to think about how our principles may conflict with people and situations. So, we pragmatically do what we need to do to get along with the world. We rationalize decisions by saying it is for the common good, or nobody really cares. In effect, we hide from the implications of our beliefs by going-along-to-get-along.

The intersection between the philosophical and the practical is the ground upon which we can answer "Who am I?" With clarity of thought about our values and purpose, we can make choices that lead us towards fulfillment and impact in our lives. This is not an either/ or question, but a both/and one. To live our lives based upon values that represent who I am is the goal.

The context of this alignment represents the two sides of the other coin. Think of this as the coin of expectation whereas the other is the coin of identity. The tension of this second coin is one of conformity. Do we conform our lives to the values and practices that define us personally? Or do we conform to the expectations of all those social groups that make claims on our time, our talent, our principles, and our resources?

Add into the mix that much of our lives are lived in reaction to people with whom we do not have a personal or direct relationship, and a kind of tyranny of the social emerges. If I am unclear about my values or my purpose, and the practice of my life is a mess, then the conflict between being the person that I desire to be and the person the crowd wants me to be becomes one of loss and isolation.

This is why the solution to these highly pressurized situations can be reduced to learning how to say No.

> No, I will not act against my principles.

> No, I will not act simply to go along with the crowd.

> No, I will not act to simply make someone else feel better.

> Yes, I will act upon the values that make sense for my life.

> Yes, I will act according to my purpose to make a difference that matters.

> Yes, I will act to bridge the social barriers that separate people into isolated tribal groups.

The point is that when we say No, we are saying Yes to some value, purpose, or relationship that matters to us. Oh, it would be nice if it was this simple. But it is not. We need to understand why we need to learn to say No. We need to learn how to make it as practical as possible.

The Beginning of Self-Understanding

At a book signing in Denver, Jennifer came up to me. She wanted to know what my book, Circle of Impact, was about. I told her that it was for people in transition. She responded, "Oh, that describes me." I asked her what she meant.

Jennifer talked about how her husband is a take-charge guy. He makes the decisions for the family. She told me this in a matter-of-fact way. She wasn't complaining. It was clear that the arrangement had worked for her throughout their marriage. Yet here she is at my table telling me that she is in transition. What did this mean?

Jennifer wants to do something that doesn't have her husband involved. Digging a little deeper she said that she wanted to know what she was capable of doing without him. I asked her if she felt this was a question of knowing who she is. She said yes.

Here is a woman in her fifties who is as normal and engaging as any woman that I have ever met. Yet, she is telling me that this relationship of dependency with her husband is no longer working for her. She doesn't want to leave him. They have not fallen out of love. It is something deeper for Jennifer. It is the question we all face of identity and self-understanding.

I asked if there was anything in her life where her husband had no necessary connection. She thought for a brief moment and then told me about an old farmhouse that her mother's family owns in Illinois. She told me that she has been thinking of going over and renovating it. I told her I thought it was a good idea.

If she decided to renovate the house, she could find herself by contributing to something her family would find meaningful.

We desire clarity about who we are. Some decisions are simple. Some are complex. If we lack clarity about what is important to us, then even the small decisions can create stress and wreak havoc upon our peace of mind.

As Rene Girard describes, we seek this insight by looking at other people. We may or may not imitate them. We certainly compare ourselves to them. We do so because we lack the self- understanding that we need to say No to an unhealthy group mindset.

I spent twenty years as an organizational consultant. Most of my projects never reached the level of fulfillment that I had hoped for at the beginning. It took me a long time to figure out why. When I did, I realized that the reason was always present before me. It had everything to do with self-understanding.

The simple way to describe the problem is that people want change, but they don't want *to* change in order to gain it. Even when they hire someone like me to come in to do problem solving and long-range planning, they want the problems to go away. They don't want to be inconvenienced by them.

This is why I say to people, "You won't change until the pain of changing is less than the pain of remaining the same." If we live a life of pain avoidance, seeking safety and security, then we are choosing to accept a more mediocre existence. To always say Yes requires no courage, but it is risky. There is a risk that comes from both facing our problems and trying to avoid them. Risk is inherent in transition. There is risk in saying No. Risk comes with trying something new, of stretching for some new understanding of oneself. There is also a risk in plunging our heads into the sand and ignoring reality. All risk is mitigated by a mindset of learning what I need to know to take the next step. Therefore, we start with small endeavors, with a simple No that helps us know what it feels like to stand up for ourselves.

At the very beginning of a change process, people need affirmation. Not the kind that says everything is okay or you are the best. Rather, we need the affirmation that it is possible to change everything in our life. When we decide to say No, and affirm the Yes of our values, we are displaying a newfound self-understanding.

What is it you truly want? What keeps you and me from achieving our deepest desires in life? Is it our fear of failing, of humiliation, of loss of status or friends, or even family? Without a clear sense of purpose, it is easy to settle for a mediocre life with all its stresses and obligations that never bring fulfillment.

Let's say we need to lose weight. Simply shifting our diet from processed foods to real food is not sufficient. We have to address the whole of our life. We have to decide that the question is about our health, not our diet. Elevating health over diet requires us to educate ourselves about our bodies, our mind, our emotions, and the spiritual center of life. The result is self- awareness. This awareness is not just about our self. It is about all that surrounds us. It is how we can know how to say No and Yes through the regimens of diet, exercise, sleep, stress management, relationships with people, and our careers.

We need to ask and answer the question about why. What is our why in relation to our talent, skills, knowledge, experience, and passion for impact? The choice we have to make is between a life that quickly passes us by without knowing what has happened – Remember, the days are long and the years are short - and a life focused on what we want to achieve with the people with whom we love and care about.

Self-understanding is where we begin. We need to know who we are, what we value, what our purpose is, and what our long-term goals are. We need to know what our strengths and our weaknesses are. We need to see that where we start in seeking to understand ourselves continues throughout our lives.

If you are a person who has responsibility for other people, as a parent or a business owner or manager, then your capacity to fulfill your responsibilities doesn't begin with your skills set, but your understanding of yourself. It is the greatest obstacle to success in life, as it is for organizations.

A Persistent, Residual Culture of Values

Early in my life, the social part of my life bewildered me. I didn't understand social relations. It wasn't that I couldn't relate to people. It was something else. It had more to do with the purpose of these relationships. During those years, I lived in my head. It was easy to do. I read a lot. Spent a lot of time thinking and reflecting upon life. That individualistic side was driven by my questions. It is what ultimately led me to questions about leadership. This long journey provided me the opportunity to strengthen the social side of my life. To better understand the importance of our networks of relationships. It was out of this long experience that the Circle of Impact model of leadership was born. I designed it to help people manage the two sides of life's coin.

I learned that culture grows out of our social relations. People are socially joined together, united into a community, through their individual contributions. The stickiness of these relationships happen as we discover the values that we share in common. Deny people the opportunity to contribute and you deny them the dignity of being a person of impact.

At the heart of our social cultures are stories. We tell them in a wide variety of ways. They are not just literal stories, but symbolic stories. We create art to tell the story of our deepest beliefs. We attend events to share the experience of the fulfillment of life. We go to a concert, the theatre, a sporting event, a wedding, a lecture, a holiday party with family members, or dinner with friends to experience togetherness. Joy, affirmation, and hope emerge in these shared experiences. In many ways, the organizations and institutions of society are born from these social lives. Together we organize to solve problems, expand our understanding of the world, and provide opportunities for self-discovery.

Traveling the world speaking and meeting people I see a common thread that transcends every distinction that categorizes us. Hidden in plain sight, in every place where people live and work together there exists *a persistent, residual culture of values.* Where you live and work right now, there exists a culture that *persists* because it *resides* in the shared values of the people in relationship with one another. This culture is not the fulfillment of an organization's strategic initiative. It emerges from the interaction of people, from their relationships.

This insight became clear to me as I was introduced to an executive assistant to a Senior Vice President of a global manufacturing company that had gone through a series of public failures. Her demeanor was very formal, almost aggressively defensive towards me. After a few moments of introduction, I said to her, "A company is not defined by its executives or its tragedies. It is defined by its people, by its persistent, residual culture of relationships. It is why you have remained here for almost three decades. It is why you love this company and why you feel pain in the midst of these hard times."

All her stiff defensiveness left as she realized that this stranger standing before her understood what thousands of her co-workers also felt.

Two Principles To Guide Us

Recently, I interviewed a group of women in rural Kenya who participate in a rural economic development training program teaching them to farm. They start with one chicken and expand to include vegetable gardening, dairy, and forestry. I asked them how the training program had impacted their families. Six months into the program, they are able to take care of themselves and their families. They don't have to go begging for help. They told me that dependency and idleness which lead to hardship and crime can now be avoided. They even spoke about saving money so that when they got old they had something to live on.

These women want to be *self-sufficient* and *interdependent*. These are the desirable goals of our two-sided coin. If we think of our lives as the tension between the personal and the social, we need a way to see where we want to be once we have brought alignment to our lives through clarity about our values.

Many people with whom I've talked aren't needing physical self-sufficiency like these women. Instead, we need mental, emotional, and spiritual self-sufficiency. I see this as simply being able to stand on our own. Self-knowledge is not a list, but a quality of presence. It is an integrated life where those four aspects of personhood blend into a whole understanding of who we are.

How do I know that we lack self-sufficiency in Western culture? Because I see how pathologic social conformity has become for people. Fear drives people's lives. I never watch televised news. The other night at a friend's house we watched a segment until I asked him to turn it off. Each story was promoting paranoia. They wanted us to feel like we don't know anything and that they know everything. They were social conditioning us to respond to everything in fear or disgust. Both are emotions that when pushed to the extreme, create emotional harm.

To be self-sufficient is to think for oneself. It means that you are capable of thinking rationally. I once would have said critically, but that type of thinking is born out of this defensive, fear- based mindset. Self-sufficient people are open-minded, embracing the whole of life, while at the same time able to say No because their values point them to Yes.

The other side of the Kenyan women's coin is *interdependency*. For them, this means that they support one another in their efforts to become *self-sufficient*. They are not alone. They are together. Interdependency is what genuine community looks like. However, this is not what I see here.

Our community relations are institutional. We relate through business-like structures that organize how we know one another. Social media platforms are no different. We are connected to one another, but not directly. Our social relations are mediated, or shall I say managed, not by our values, but by algorithms that determine who receives our posts and what information is available to us. This system is not for our benefit, but for the companies that own these social media companies. While our participation is voluntary, it is not free. It is a system that promotes social dependency, not *interdependency*. It comes at a high cost.

An *interdependent* relationship is measured in the same way the relationship dimension of the Circle of Impact model is. We seek relationships of *respect, trust,* and *mutual accountability*.

How do we know what this is like? It is a vitally important question. For if our social

relationships are mediated for institutional purposes, then we don't have a relationship but a connection. One that does not provide an environment for a direct experience of respect, trust, and mutual accountability. Those are qualities of direct relationships, not social media connections. It is an important distinction.

The principles of *self-sufficiency* and *interdependency* provide us a way to live our lives so that we can say No. Where we find social dependency, we find a loss of *self-sufficiency*. If we are not free to say No, then we are not free to treat people with respect, trust, and mutual accountability. Instead, we are obliged to conform to the social environment that is managing us. We are socially dependent.

Values, the Key To Turning No's to Yes'

The two sides of the personal/social coin are found here. Where one side or the other is broken, we are broken. In this brokenness, we either have lost our sense of identity or we have lost the social relationships where we find affirmation, nurture, and support. We are not just individuals and we are not just mass consumers of products and culture. We are human beings whose lives are only complete when we have a defined purpose for impact that can operate within the social culture of shared values.

We need values that define us. We don't shop for values as if they are commodities on a shelf. Instead, our values reveal themselves to us as we live. We'll only discover them if we are open to finding them.

In my book *Circle of Impact: Taking Personal Initiative To Ignite Change*, I tell the story of my summer in 1981 as a volunteer refugee worker in Pakistan. Our work was to travel throughout the northern mountain regions looking for small encampments of refugees. They were mostly Afghans who had fled their country's war with the Soviet Union. One of the camps we found was on a dry, dusty plain outside Peshawar. After providing food, clothing, and some new tents to the refugees, one man came up to me. He took my hands. Cupped them between his and shook them. Then he reached up and stroked my beard. Later our host, Gordon, told me that the man had thanked me by honoring me as one Afghan man does to another.

I had never been thanked in such a way before. I had never been treated with honor. At that moment, I knew that honor was the value that would define my life. What does that mean? It means that I must live honorably with integrity, respect, trust, and gratitude towards others. This is not the honor of forced loyalty. Violate the family's honor and you get whacked. Rather, this is the honor of dignity.

Honor is how the two sides of my coin come together. I was prepared to receive honor because of how I was raised. The society of my family created a receptivity to see the Afghan man's expression of honor as a life-defining experience. Let me explain.

When I was eleven or twelve years old, my mother's mother, whom we called Grandmere, told me,

> "You can do anything you want, but do
> not bring shame to the family name."

I've told this story often because it describes the culture of my family and defines the social expectations that came with it. To this day, at times of decision, I ponder, "What would

Grandmere think?" Our family, both my father's and my mother's, lived in a culture of ancestral remembrance and honor. For my siblings, my children, and my cousins, we recognize that we are not just individuals passing through this moment in time. We are members of a family extending many generations back in time.

I have enjoyed how people have responded to the story of my grandmother's cautionary words to me. Usually, people laugh because it feels so archaic. How many people do you know who would refrain from some action because shame presents a positive boundary for their behavior? Not very many I suspect. It is very old school. If you knew my grandmother it would make perfect sense. She invented old school. I love her and my grandfather for it because it has rooted our family in time, not just the present, but historical time. My father always joked about our family practicing ancestry worship. It really isn't that. It is more akin to William Faulkner's thought expressed in his novel *Requiem for a Nun*, "*The past is not dead. It isn't even past.*" For my family, our ancestors are still with us. Their example establishes a guide for how we should live that is captured well in my grandmother's comment to me.

The other response to her comment is a negative reaction to feeling personally bound to someone else's expectation of us. How many parents have heard their child say to them, "Don't tell me how I should live my life!" My grandmother's admonition to me is seen as an unfair obstacle for me to overcome. What you must understand is that I don't see it as archaic or personally binding. It is rather where my freedom to pursue my life has come. My grandmother did not tell me that because she wanted to restrict my life. She said it because she saw something in me that needed a set of boundaries in order for me to find real fulfillment. I honor her thought as an act of love. It is why I dedicate this book to her.

If we are learning to say No based on the Yes's of our values, then we need to dig deeper into understanding who we are. This is the gift my family gave me. In return, I share with others.

A curious trend emerged over the past decade. People began to personally brand themselves. The platforms of social media, like Instagram, TikTok, and YouTube became outlets for projecting the personality of individuals onto the screens of millions of people worldwide. For the first time in human history, the average person can turn their personal identity into a marketable persona generating significant income.

A dozen years ago I entered an online contest. As fortune would have it, I became one of the finalists. The task for me was to generate votes for my four-word answer to the question at the center of the contest. The experience changed my life because I had to market myself as an online personality. I did not win the contest, which is another story altogether. What it showed me was that there is a difference between my personal identity and a marketable personal brand.

A few years later as I prepared to publish *Circle of Impact: Taking Personal Initiative to Ignite Change*, I realized that I am ill-suited for a time where self-promotion and personal branding are how we measure a person's value. I am not an "on-air" personality. Rather, I am an average guy who thinks deeply and cares about people. As a result, I am at a loss to tell you what my personal brand is. However, I can tell you who I am, where I came from, where I am going, what I believe and value, my purpose, and the goals for my life and work. Instead of a marketing persona, I am a real person.

Therefore, let's not speak of a personal brand. Because I believe it is a poor substitute for real self-knowledge. If you need to brand yourself, call a marketer. If you need to discover how to live a life where you can always say Yes to the things that matter to you, and No to ones that don't, then stick with me. We can travel this journey of discovery together. Can I get a Yes to that?

References and Comments

Circle of Impact: Taking Personal Initiative To Ignite Change – Dr. Ed Brenegar

https://amazon.com/author/edbrenegar

Rene' Girard

https://en.wikipedia.org/wiki/Ren%C3%A9_Girard

Rene' Girard's work is insightful because he sees how humans are not born programmed to act a certain way. We learn by imitating others.

> "We don't even know what our desire is. We ask other people to tell us our desires. We would like our desires to come from our deepest selves, our personal depths - but if it did, it would not be desire. Desire is always for something we feel we lack."

"A mimetic crisis is when people become undifferentiated. There are no more social classes, there are no more social differences, and so forth."

"What I call a mimetic crisis is a situation of conflict so intense that on both sides people act the same way and talk the same way even though, or because, they are more and more hostile to each other."

Girard points to the situation we all face where we want to be like others and at the same time be different. The real question that we face is between the absolute individual and the absolute social conformist. The path towards an answer is to think for yourself, to be self-critical, and establish a level of self-awareness that avoids our relationships turning violent.

This five part interview of Rene' Girard by David Cayley of the CBC is a good introduction.

Audio: http://www.davidcayley.com/podcasts/category/Ren%C3%A9+Girard Transcript: http://www.davidcayley.com/s/Scapegoat.PDF

Charles Taylor
https://en.wikipedia.org/wiki/Charles_Taylor_(philosopher)

The ideas on first and second-order desires come from an essay *What is Human Agency?* in Human Agency and Language: Philosophical Papers 1 by Charles Taylor. The idea of a human agency is about how we are individuals who make decisions and take action for specific reasons. All animals desire food. As human agents, we can not only distinguish between the foods we like and dislike, and also can say whether the steak this time was as good as the last time we visited the restaurant. We are individual agents of thought, choice, and action. Taylor writes.

> "What is it that we attribute to ourselves as human agents which we would not attribute to animals? …
>
> The key notion is the distinction between first- and second-order desires … I can be said to have a second-order desire when I have a desire whose object is my having a certain (first-order) desire. …
>
> Put in other terms, we think of … animals as having desires, even as having to choose between desires in some cases, or at least as inhibiting some desires for the sake of others. But what is distinctively human is the power to *evaluate* our desires, to regard some as desirable and others are undesirable. This is why

'no animal other than man … appears to have the capacity for reflective self- evaluation that is manifested in the formation of second-order desires.'" p.15-16.

The importance for us is that you and I are not machines or simple animals who do things by instinct or programming. We think. We feel. We discern. We choose. We act. All those are important for establishing our sense of individual identity. This is why we need to discern how places of social engagement, like social media platforms, can function to deny us our capacity to treat our second-order desires with respect. To have clear second-order desires is to be able to know our minds and live with purpose and meaning.

Who is Dr. Ed Brenegar?

Dr. Ed Brenegar is a global thought leader, trainer, speaker, and networker. His purpose is to inspire and equip people world-wide to take personal initiative to create impact for their local communities. He has created the Circle of Impact Institute to expand his impact through his writing and training. He is the author of *Circle of Impact: Taking Personal Initiative To Ignite Change*. He is the Founder and Facilitator of the Global Impact Network whose purpose is the establishment and support local networks of relationships on a global scale.

Circle of Impact Institute:

Publications

> *Circle of Impact: Taking Personal Initiative to Ignite Change* Translations: English, Chinese (Mandarin), Arabic

> *Circle of Impact Africa* – English, French

21st Century Leadership Guide series

Leading For Impact weblog – https://edbrenegar.com/blog

Training

Impact Day Consultation - Planning / Problem Solving for Individuals and Groups

Circle of Impact Introduction Video Series - Free

Advanced Circle of Impact Training Video Series – Fee-based

Global Impact Network:

Network of Relationships Training

Facilitation for Formation and Development of local networks for impact

Contact Information:

Dr. Ed Brenegar
Circle of Impact, LLC.
ed@edbrenegar.com
+1-828-275-1803
https://edbrenegar.com

www.ingramcontent.com/pod-product-compliance
Lightning Source LLC
Chambersburg PA
CBHW071501070426
42452CB00041B/2085